The Classical Piano
Sheet Music Series

INTERMEDIATE
CLASSICAL ERA
FAVORITES

ISBN 978-1-7051-2475-8

Copyright © 2021 by HAL LEONARD LLC
International Copyright Secured All Rights Reserved

Visit Hal Leonard Online at
www.halleonard.com

Contact us:
Hal Leonard
7777 West Bluemound Road
Milwaukee, WI 53213
Email: info@halleonard.com

In Europe, contact:
Hal Leonard Europe Limited
42 Wigmore Street
Marylebone, London, W1U 2RN
Email: info@halleonardeurope.com

In Australia, contact:
Hal Leonard Australia Pty. Ltd.
4 Lentara Court
Cheltenham, Victoria, 3192 Australia
Email: info@halleonard.com.au

Contents

Minuet in G Major
WoO 10, No. 2

Ludwig van Beethoven
(1770–1827)

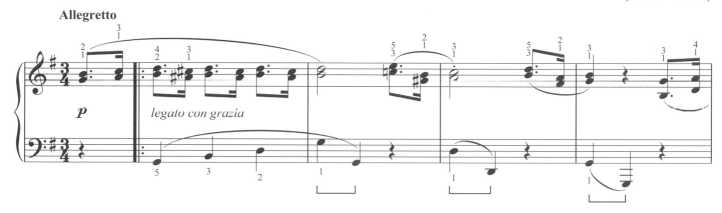

TRIO

Contradance in C Major
WoO 14, No. 1

Ludwig van Beethoven
(1770–1827)

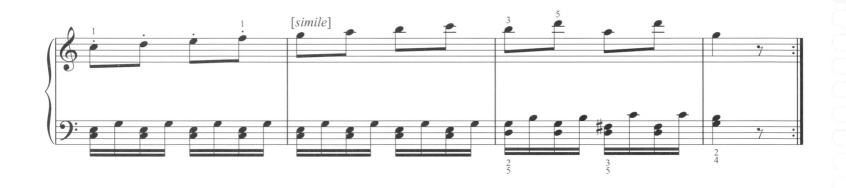

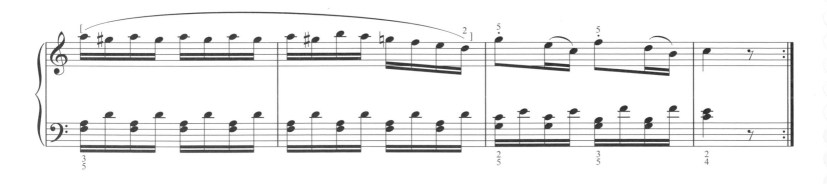

Ecossaise in G Major
WoO 23

Ludwig van Beethoven
(1770–1827)
transcribed by Carl Czerny

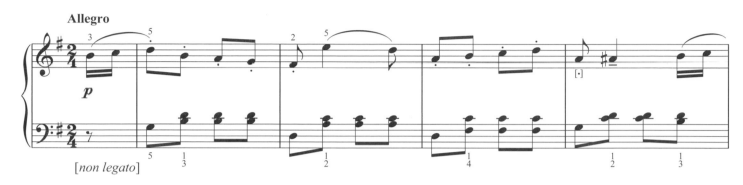

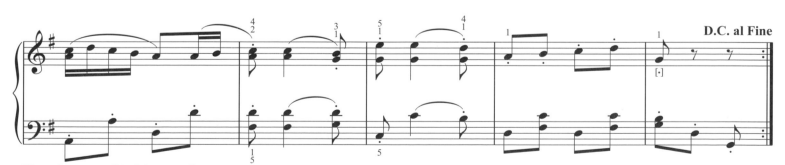

Fingerings are editorial suggestions.

German Dance in G Major

WoO 8, No. 6

Ludwig van Beethoven
(1770–1827)

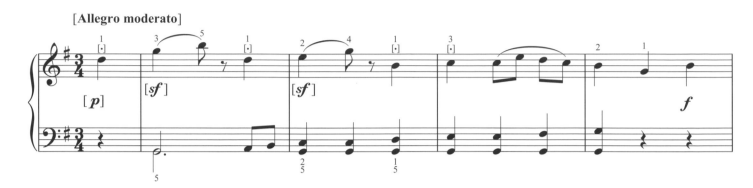

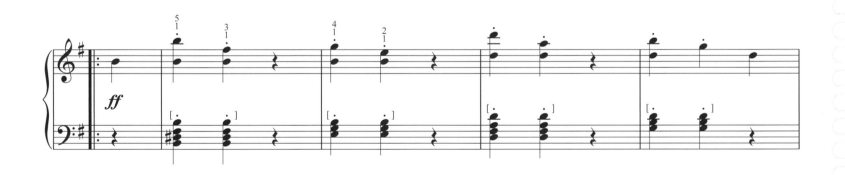

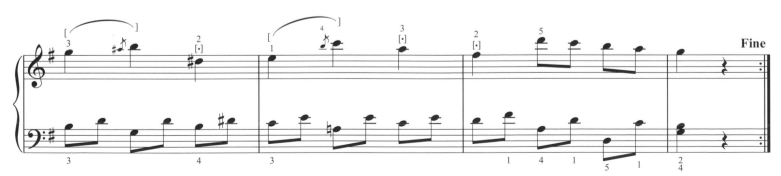

Editorial suggestions are in brackets.

D.C. al Fine
senza repetizione

German Dance in C Major

WoO 8, No. 7

Ludwig van Beethoven
(1770–1827)

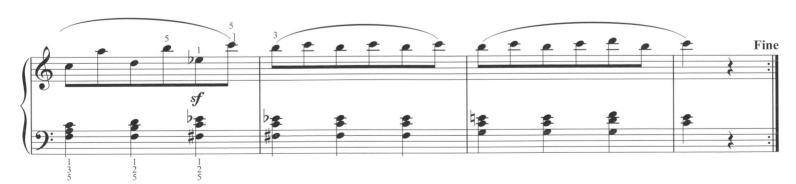

Editorial suggestions are in brackets.

Trio

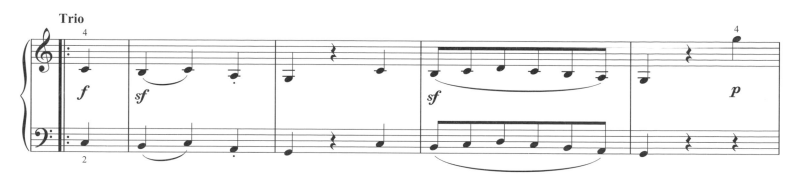

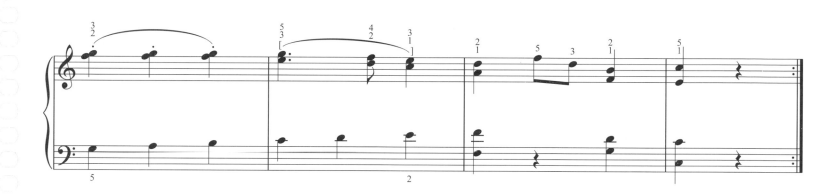

D.C. al Fine
senza repetizione

German Dance in B-flat Major
WoO 13, No. 2

Ludwig van Beethoven
(1770–1827)

[Allegro moderato]

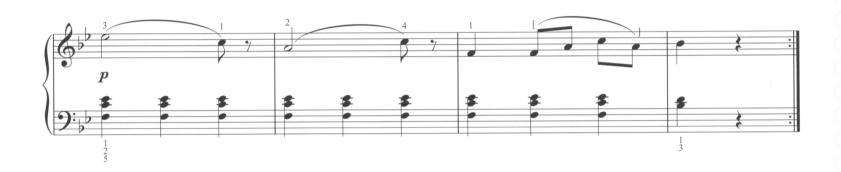

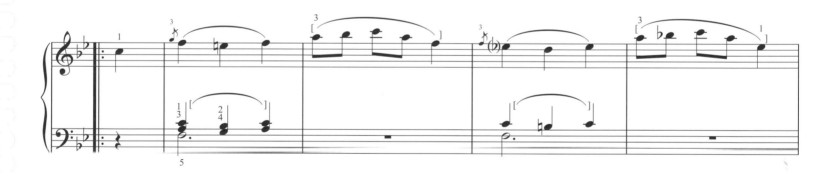

D.C. al Fine
senza repetizione

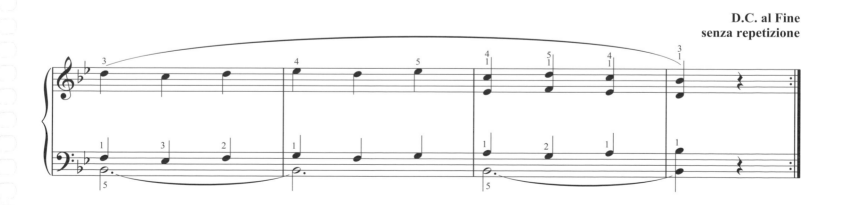

Sonatina in G Major

Anh. 5, No. 1

I

Ludwig van Beethoven
(1770–1827)

Editorial suggestions are in brackets.

II

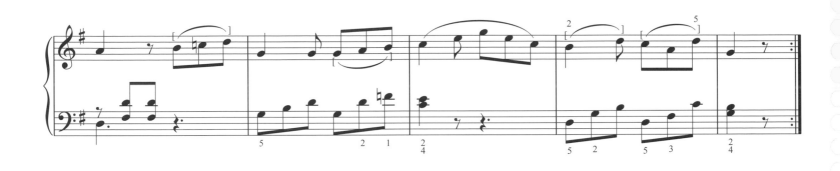

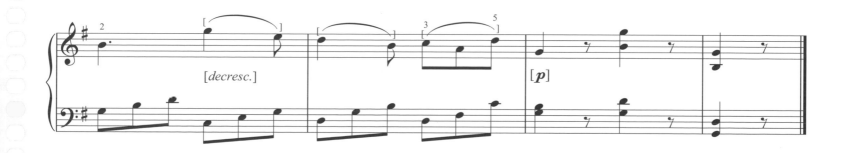

Sonatina in C Major
Op. 36, No. 1

I

Muzio Clementi
(1752–1832)

II

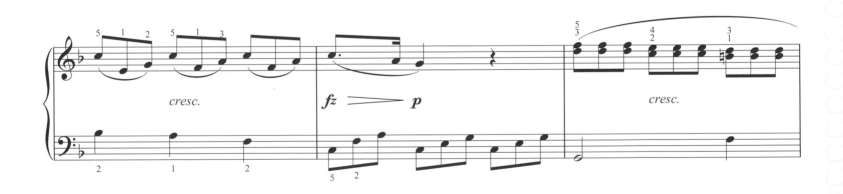

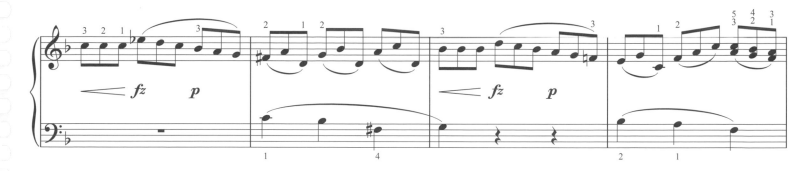

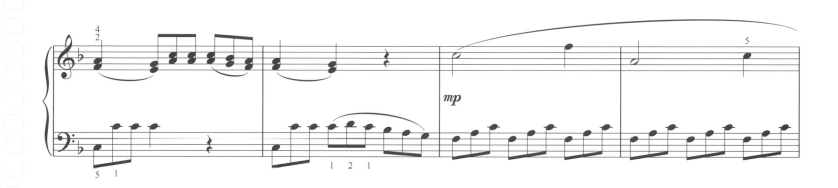

III

Sonatina in C Major

Op. 36, No. 3

I

Muzio Clementi
(1752–1832)

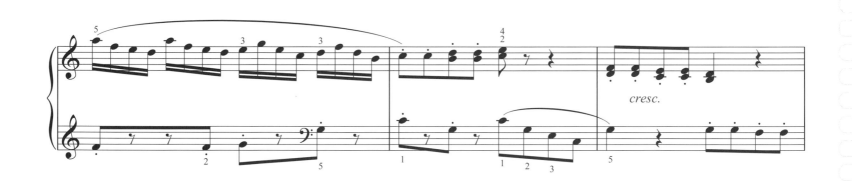

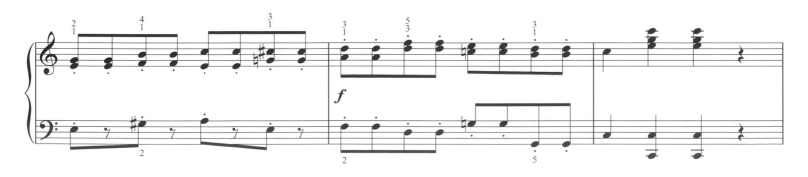

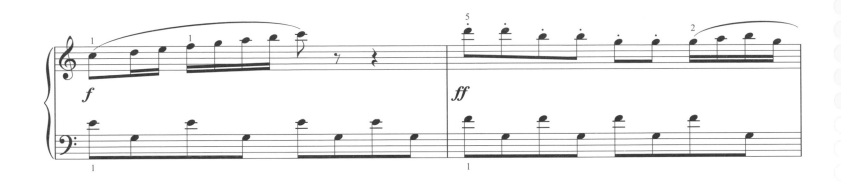

II

Un poco adagio [♩ = 72-88]

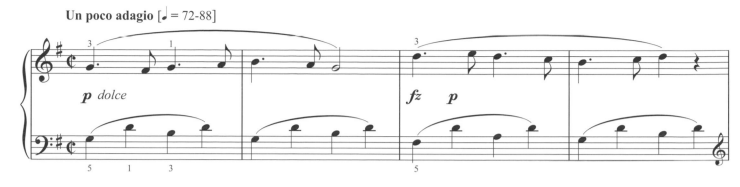

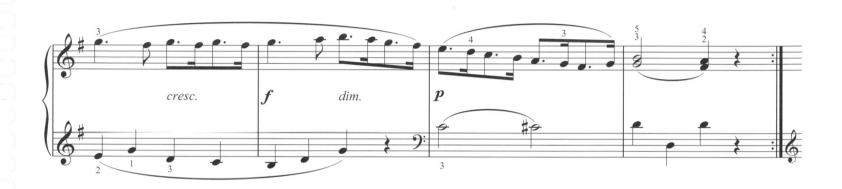

III

Sonatina in G Major
Op. 151, No. 1

I

Anton Diabelli
(1781–1858)

Andante cantabile

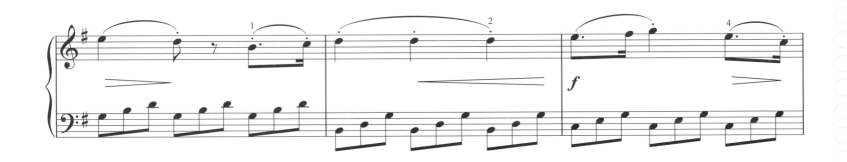

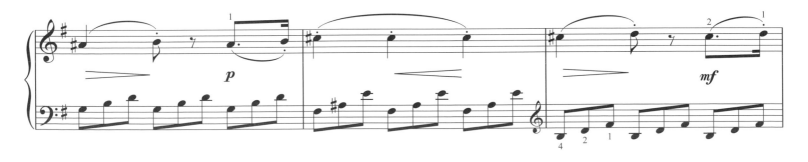

legato

II

Scherzo

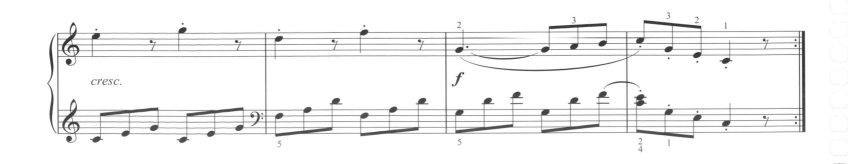

III

Rondo
Allegretto

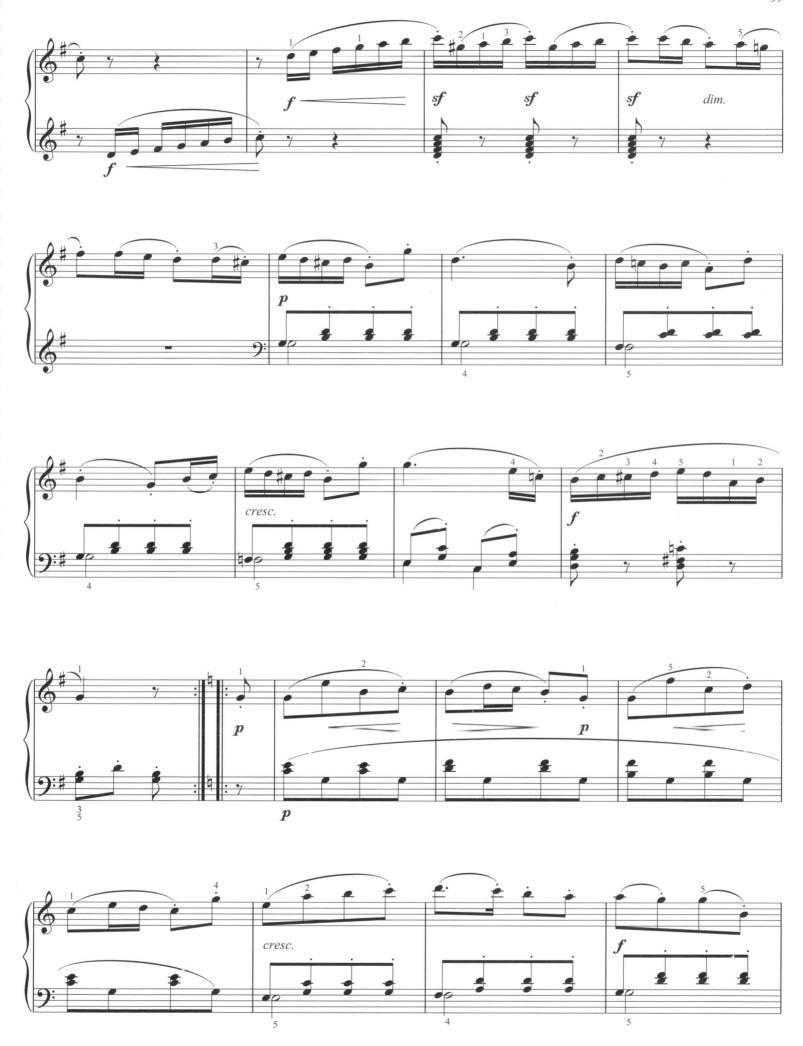

Sonatina in C Major
Op. 168, No. 3
I

Anton Diabelli
(1781–1858)

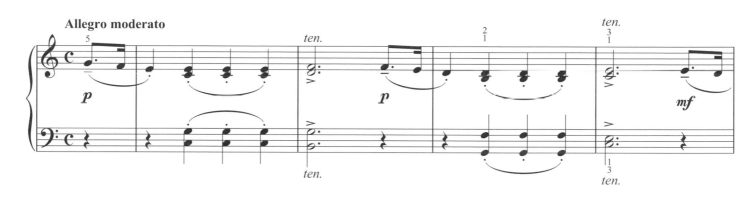

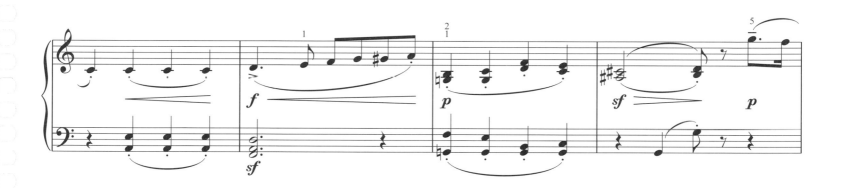

II

III

RONDO

Allegro

legato

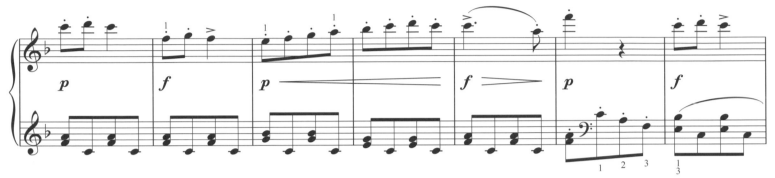

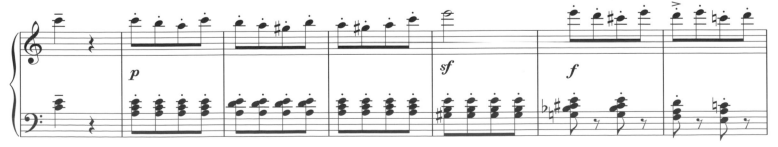

Sonatina in G Major
Op. 20, No. 1

I

Jan Ladislav Dussek
(1760–1812)

Allegro non tanto [♩ = 132]

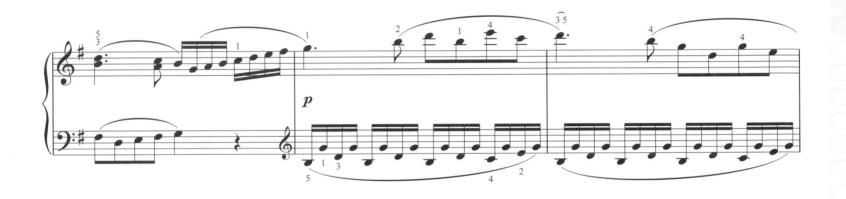

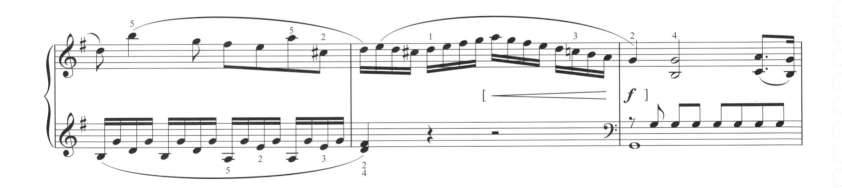

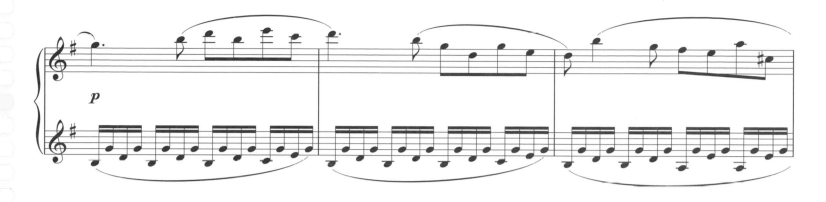

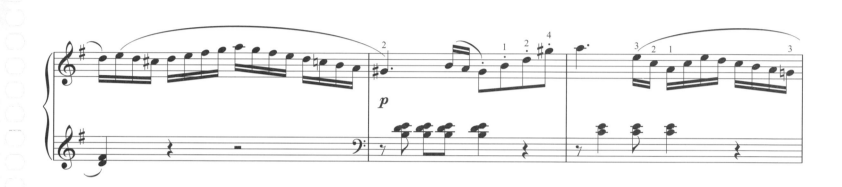

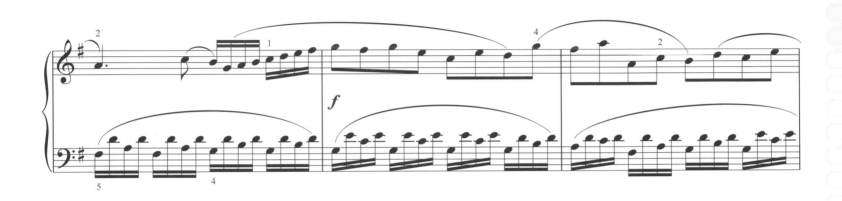

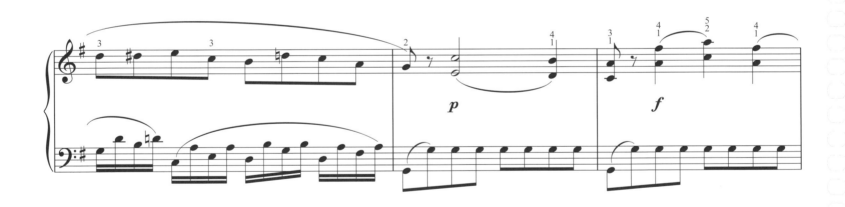

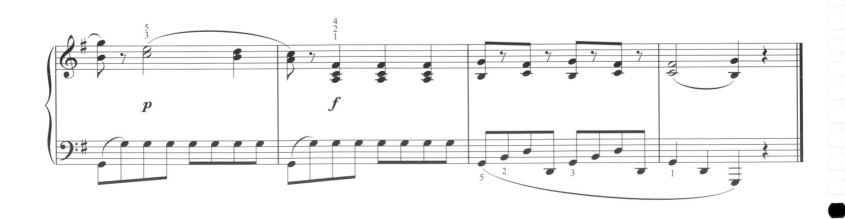

II

RONDO

Allegretto–Tempo di Minuetto [♪ = 126]

Allegro

from Sonata in C Major, Hob. XVI/1

Franz Joseph Haydn
(1732–1809)

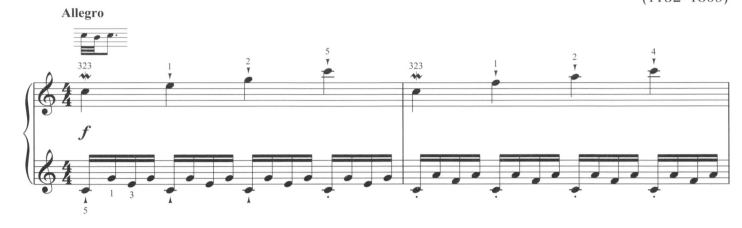

Arietta

from Variations in E-flat Major, Hob. XVII/3

Franz Joseph Haydn
(1732–1809)

Sonatina in C Major
Op. 55, No. 1
I

Friedrich Kuhlau
(1786–1832)

Allegro [♩ = ca. 88]

Editorial suggestions are in brackets.

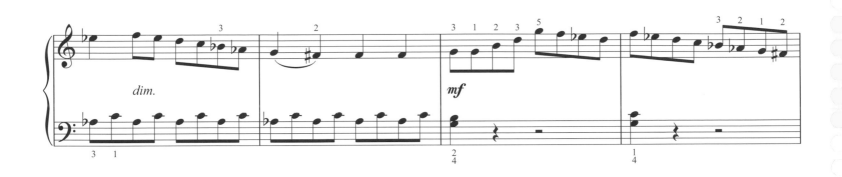

II

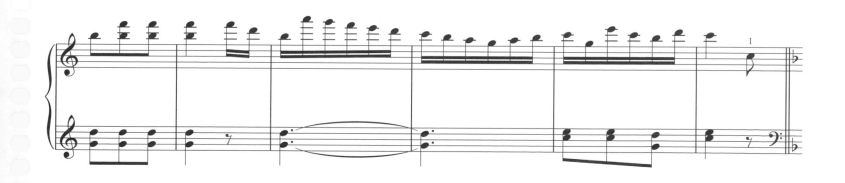

Sonatina in C Major
Op. 55, No. 3
I

Friedrich Kuhlau
(1786–1832)

Allegro con spirito [♩ = 132]

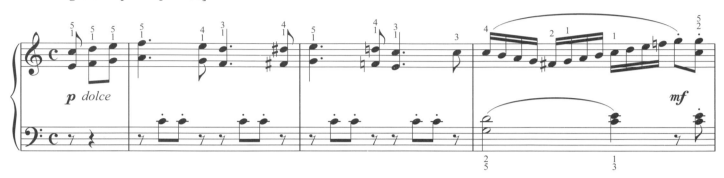

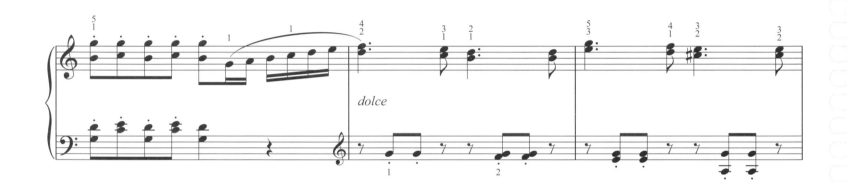

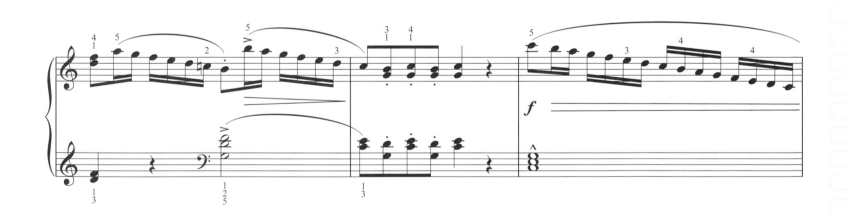

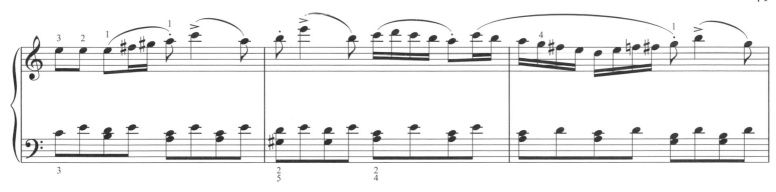

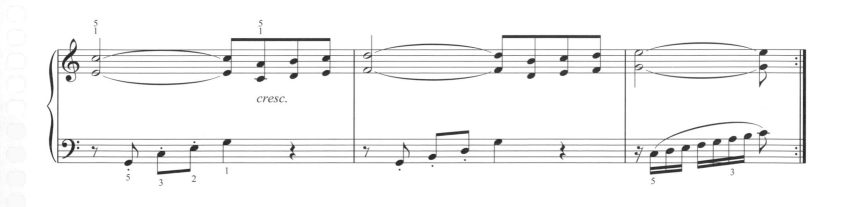

II

Allegretto grazioso [♩ = 126]

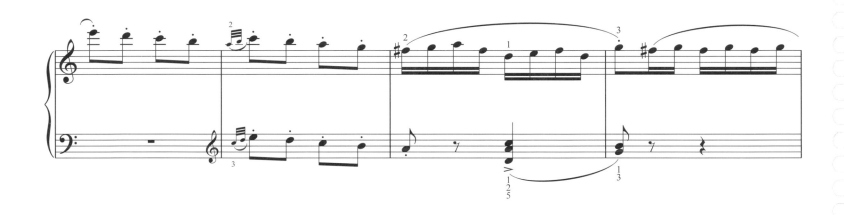

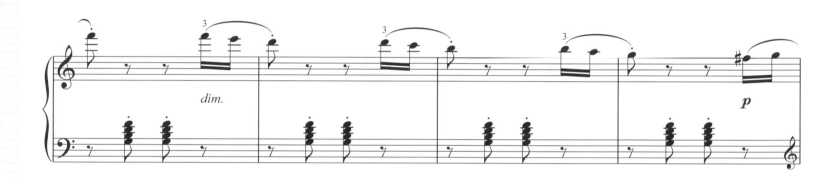

Adagio for Glass Harmonica
K. 356 (617a)

Wolfgang Amadeus Mozart
(1756–1791)

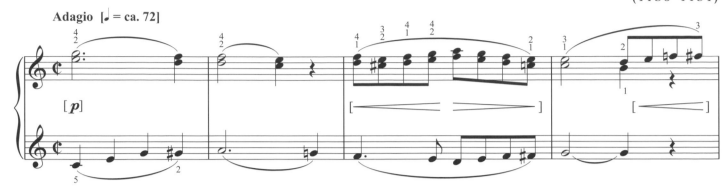

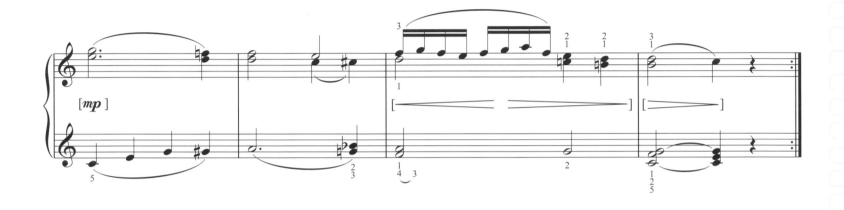

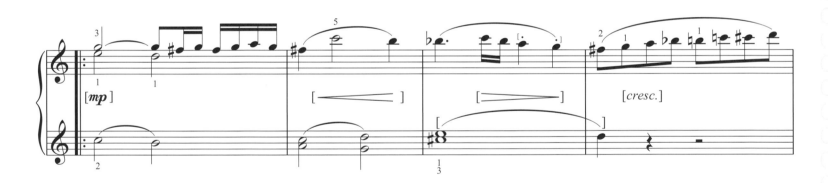

Editorial suggestions are in brackets.

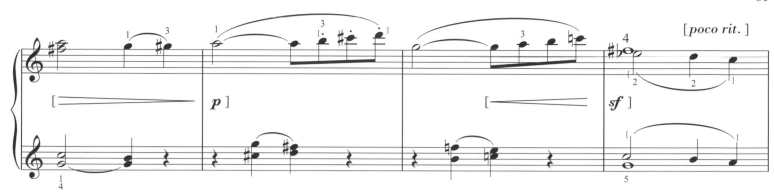

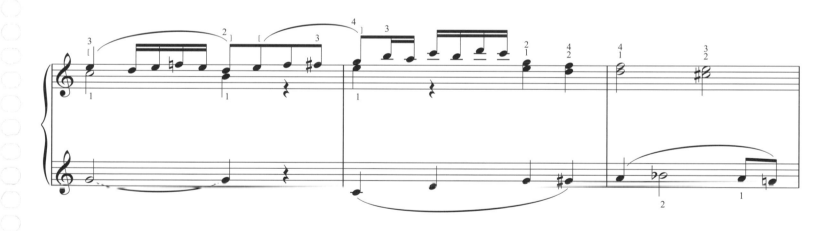

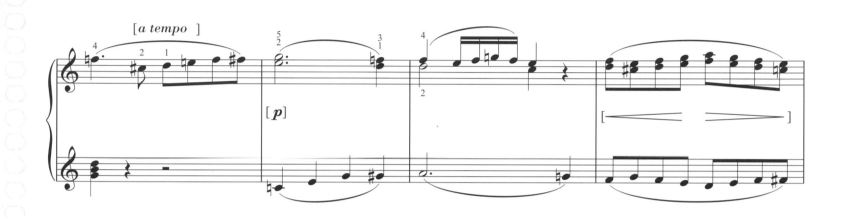

Andantino in E-flat Major

Adaptation of an aria* by Christoph Willibald Gluck, K. 236 (588b)

Wolfgang Amadeus Mozart
(1756–1791)

* "Non vi turbate" from *Alceste*.
Editorial suggestions are in brackets.

Contradance in G Major
K. 15e

Wolfgang Amadeus Mozart
(1756–1791)

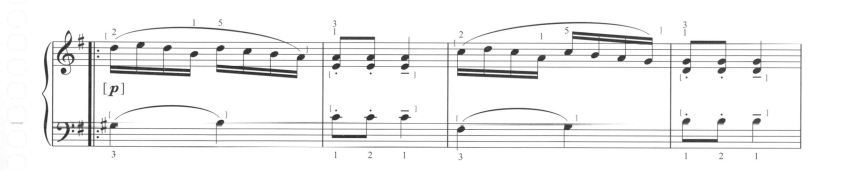

Funeral March for
Signor Maestro Contrapunto

K. 453a

Wolfgang Amadeus Mozart
(1756–1791)

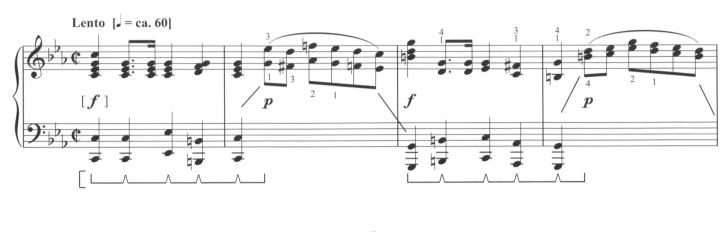

Fingerings are editorial suggestions.

Allegro

from Sonata in C Major, K. 545 ("Sonata facile")

Wolfgang Amadeus Mozart
(1756–1791)

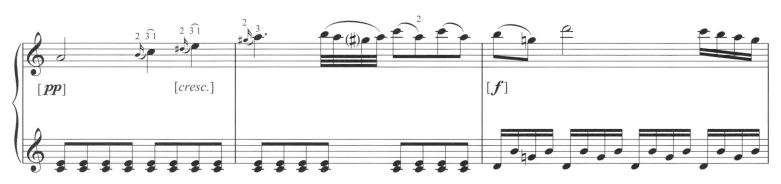

German Dance in C Major
K. 605, No. 3

Wolfgang Amadeus Mozart
(1756–1791)

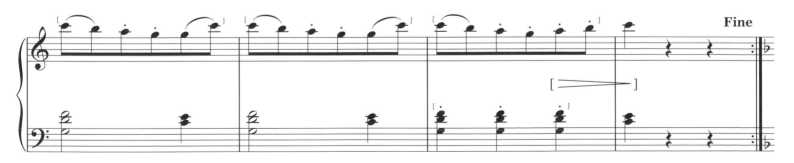

Eliminate repeats on the Da Capo.
Editorial suggestions are in brackets.

Trio (The Sleighride)

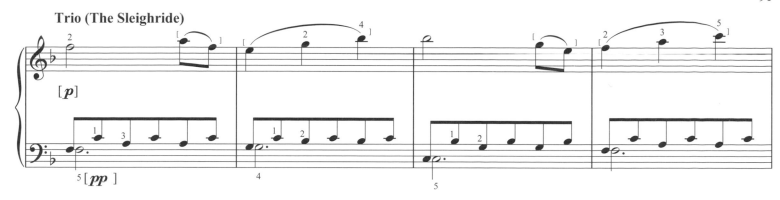

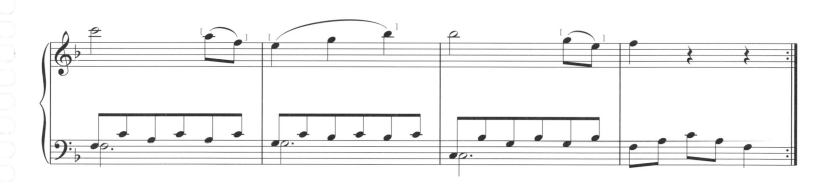

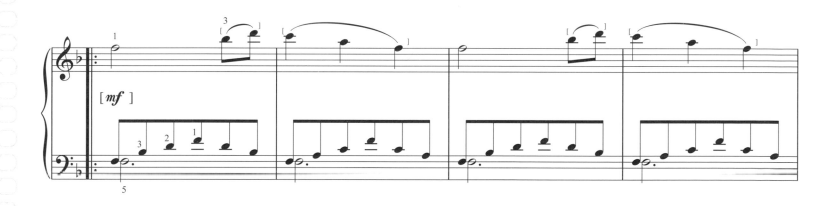

**D.C. al Fine
second time**

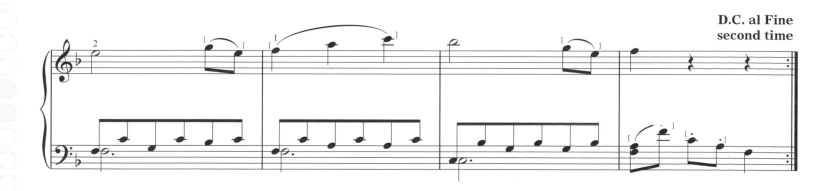

Piece for Clavier in F Major
K. 33B

Wolfgang Amadeus Mozart
(1756–1791)

Editorial suggestions are in brackets.

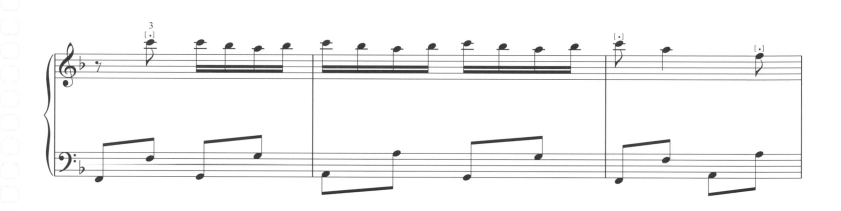

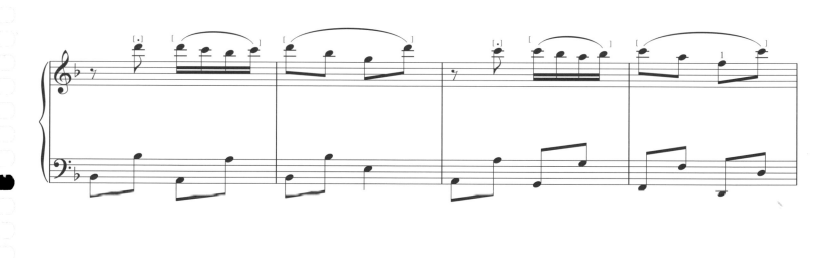

[*poco rit. 2nd time*]

Rondo in C Major
K. 334 (320b)

Wolfgang Amadeus Mozart
(1756–1791)

Editorial suggestions are in brackets.